God Speaks

Prophetic Words and Visions from Abba's Heart

Vol. I

Edie Bayer

Available in This Series:

God Speaks: Prophetic Words
and Visions from Abba's Heart
Vol. I and Vol. II
ISBN-13: 978-1-946106-26-1
ISBN-13: 978-1-946106-27-8

Other books by Edie Bayer:

Spiritual Espionage: Going Undercover for the Kingdom of God!
Power Thieves: 7 Spirits that Steal Your Power, and How to Get it Back!
Spiritual Lightning Rods Connected to the Father of Lights
Narco: Awake O' Sleeper
Write That Book! You Have a Book in You – Now Write It!
Book and Workbook

CD's and DVD's
Salt – Cd/Dvd
Write That Book! – Cd/Dvd

http://KingdomPromoters.org/books_cds.html

Watch our Author Seminar Online 24/7:
http://KingdomPromoters.org/writerclass.html

Copyright © 2017 Edie Bayer
All rights reserved.
Printed in USA
ISBN: 1-946106-26-7
ISBN-13: 978-1-946106-26-1

DEDICATION

To my friend, Darren Canning, who
convinced me to do what I teach to others.

God Speaks

CONTENTS

	Acknowledgments	i
1	It Is Time To Catch The Rose Of Sharon	1
2	Amos 9 – It's Harvest Time	5
3	God Is Building, Fashioning And Molding	9
4	Marching Through The Door To More. Get In Order According To Matthew 12:34! Go Supernatural	13
5	I Heard A Voice Say: "Follow Me!"	19
6	God Is Moving Us To A New Place	23
7	Stages	27
8	The Action Center and a Pattern for Revival	33
9	God Is Giving Us Bundles Of Blessings!	39
10	Singularity – Three Headlights	41

God Speaks

ACKNOWLEDGMENTS

Thank you Steve Shulz and Elijah List staff. You guys make my life awesome, and were instrumental in helping to form and shape Kingdom Promoters Ministry!

Thank you Joel Yount and Spirit Fuel. You are my wonderful next-gen friend.

Jo Ellen Stevens, you are my all-time favorite prophet! I am your biggest fan.

All of you have helped to contribute to this book in some way, whether you were aware of it or not.

My biggest shout-out is to my husband, Darryl Bayer, without whom this book would be impossible. I love you, Honey!

God Speaks

CHAPTER ONE

It Is Time To Catch The Rose Of Sharon

A Dream of the King with His Queen

I had a dream in the early hours of the morning recently. In it I am a watcher, as if I am watching "a movie". There is a King and Queen dancing in a dark room, wearing clothing that is reminiscent of a long-gone era, however is not time specific. During their formal dance, their two bodies are separated by some space. His right hand is on her waist. She has long brown hair, loose and flowing down her back. He is wearing His crown and has a square jaw. As they slowly dance, she has her right hand in His left and she holds her dress in her left hand as they dance. There is a sense of intimacy between them that is established over time.

They dance behind a dark, wooden set of stairs, steps that seem as if they lead to an attic, but are out of sight in my dream. Suddenly, from behind the stairway, I see His hand tossing a cut-glass vase with red roses in it up the stairway. Interestingly, there are many, many roses crammed into the vase, yet only the rose blossoms are visible. The vase rolls down the steps and the Queen catches them on the third step from the bottom of the stairs. In the dream it seems important that the roses are caught by the Queen... and she does.

Then the "camera" cuts to a close up of the King's left hand. In the area between the thumb and first finger there is a red wound, as if he has been scratched by a finger nail. The "camera" then moves to just one section of his jaw, and there is a wound on his jaw as well. The "camera" then shows a very tight close-up of the Queen's face to focus on a scar that is hidden in her eyebrow. There are also some other scars on her face and forehead, as if she has been cut while fighting in the past and they have healed over time. Some of these scars are larger and deeper than the others. Most are healed, but there are cuts on her face that are still raw and red.

In this dream I see the beautiful imagery of the end-time Church. I see the King, our King Jesus, who is dancing with His beloved Bride, His Queen. She is beautiful, but she bears the scars of the many hits she has taken to her face. The enemy has tried to "de-face" the Church, to make her less attractive and beautiful. She bears the battle scars of multiple fights over time, some obvious, and some not so obvious... such as the one hidden in the eyebrow of the beautiful Queen.

Interpretation: The Bride Will Catch Her Rose of Sharon!

In spite of her scars, our King loves her still, and offers her flowers – ROSES – in a cut-glass vase. He is offering Himself to her, for He is the Rose of Sharon (Song of Solomon 2:1). The simple, wooden attic steps represent our climb to Heaven, literally a stairway to Heaven, made out of old, dark wood. Wood is symbolic of that which is dead, i.e., the old man (John 15:6). He tosses the roses up the stairs, and they roll down to the third step, where the Bride catches them.

This is important, because we have already had two great

awakenings and there is yet one more to come! This time the Queen, His beloved, will "CATCH" the Rose of Sharon!

The cuts and scars on the King are symbolic as well. He has obviously "taken one on the jaw", however undoubtedly turned the other cheek (Matthew 5:39). In addition, our King has a wound on His left hand. The first finger is indicative of God, the number "1" power and authority. The thumb stands for our "will". One is helpless without thumbs, and cannot exert his own will, which is why thumbs are removed from captured Bible kings (Judges 1:6-7). In addition, blood and/or oil is applied to the thumbs to set a priest apart for service to God (Exodus 29:20, Leviticus 14:7).

In my dream, the King bears a wound on His left hand – the left symbolizing the supernatural and the right symbolizing the natural. This shows an attempt by the enemy to destroy the power, authority, holiness and the Will of God in this earth realm. The good news... it's just a scratch! The enemy has failed! He has failed to take off the King's thumb and forefinger, and has failed to remove His power, authority and His will! His holiness remains (Amos 4:2, Hebrews 12:10)!

Our Queen holds her garb – her clothes of righteousness — with her left hand, while the King holds her right hand in His left. Her garb is held – dictated – by "the supernatural", as she decrees a thing and it shall surely come to pass (Job 22:28). She puts on her garment of praise (Isaiah 61:3) while He holds her natural circumstances in His supernatural hands (John 10:29)! He holds her body gently by the waist, steering her as they dance, both leading and guiding her by the power of His Holy Spirit (John 16:13). He is unable to lose control of her in this manner, as he holds her both "in the natural" and in "the supernatural"!

This dream is a picture of what was, what is, and what is coming. Our King is guiding us and steering us both in the natural and in the supernatural. I believe we are on

the verge of the great awakening. Our King is dancing with us, leading us and guiding us into all Truth. During this end-time harvest, this time the Bride will surely CATCH her Rose of Sharon!

CHAPTER TWO

Amos 9 – It's Harvest Time!

God has been speaking to me about fruit for quite some time now. I have been in the book of Daniel for several days, but this morning the Lord said "Get out of the book of Daniel!" The next book that I opened to was Amos, and the Lord said, "Yes, Amos 8." As we all know, 8 is the number of new beginnings, and not surprisingly, although I chuckled when I saw it, the first verse talks about ripe fruit, so I knew it was confirmation.

In that verse, Amos 8:1, God asked Amos a question, a simple question, which in turn Amos answered with what he saw – a basket of fruit ... ripe, summer fruit. The next thing the Lord says seems completely unconnected, which was, "The end has come upon My people Israel; I will not pass by and spare them anymore." Knowing that God would clear up the mystery and make His intentions known, I continued on. I finished the remainder of Amos 8, and when my eyes fell upon Amos 9, I heard the Lord breathe, "THE HARVEST!"

Personally, I have been having a little difficulty hearing God for prophetic words, not one-on-one as in a conference setting and giving a personal prophetic word, but words like this one – a corporate word, one that is applicable to many people simultaneously. It's not that I can't HEAR God, I can. It's just that there was a dry spell – i.e., a FAMINE – and as Amos 8:11 says, not a famine for food, but a famine "for hearing the words of the Lord". I desperately desired to hear a corporate word from God, yet there was not one forthcoming.

Why?

I believe that God was leading me to this place, the place of ripe, summer fruit - the place of HARVEST. As a prophet, my fruit is the Word of the Lord, the prophetic word from the throne room of Grace. I have been struggling to hear the Lord, and it was work, but work with no FRUIT – nothing was coming from the Great IAM. It's been going on for a while now, a couple of months and has been very frustrating. Each time I opened the Word I asked Him for a word, yet, still nothing. I believe that He allowed me to walk through this so that you will know that NOW is your Harvest Time, that even if it seemed as if the last little bit of time was so hard, so excruciatingly hard, that all new beginnings require work – in order to receive the HARVEST.

In this case, as a sign of DOUBLE HARVEST in Amos 9:9, the Lord says that He will sift you – me, us – as grain is sifted in a sieve, yet the least kernel shall not fall upon the earth and be lost from His sight. Just this morning, as I was still asking Him for a prophetic word, I said, "Lord, if there is anything in me that is blocking your word, please show it to me!" Believe me, that is a prayer that He wants to hear, and an answer that He wants to give to you! In my case, he led me to Amos 8 and 9 – for YOU!

He has His eye on you! He is allowing things to happen in this new season, but HE IS DOING IT. It is not the enemy, it is the Lord. The reason, my friends, is that He is watchful, because He says that, "ALL THE SINNERS OF MY PEOPLE shall die by the SWORD...(Amos 8:10)" He is making your sins die by the word, His Word. He is sifting the impurities out of your life, and causing your sins to die by the Sword – the Word of God!

Years ago I was an intercessor at a deliverance conference held at a local church here. One morning of the conference, I arrived to see the building covered in vultures! Literally hundreds of vultures had assembled themselves on the peaks and rooftop of the church building. It was an awesome and eerie sight, and I have to admit, rather intimidating, causing a lot of people to be scared. Many of us thought that something terrible was going to happen to us in the conference, and the vultures were there to eat our dead corpses! Why else would there be hundreds of vultures waiting?

Leadership assembled us together and came to tell us that it was a SIGN -- in the spirit, there were many dying spiritual deaths and many spirits had to leave. The vultures were there to consume the spirits as they were leaving the building!

In the same way, you have and may still be undergoing a type of "spiritual death" in order for the Lord to release the HARVEST to you that He wants to release. He is cleansing you, fine tuning you, removing the last little specks and wrinkles.

But Good News! He says in Amos 9:13 that the plowman is overtaking the reaper! ACCELERATION! What would have taken years before is now happening in real time! The Amplified says, "…(that is, everything heretofore barren and unfruitful shall overflow with spiritual blessing). That, my friend, is where you are headed, to a time of unprecedented fruitfulness that is overflowing with goodness and blessing! God promises in verse 15, "And I will plant them upon their land, and they shall no more be torn up out of their land which I gave them, says the Lord your God."

Your land is here! The promises of God are here! Whether it is in business, ministry, relationships or whatever – it's HERE! It will be fruitful, and no man will be able to pluck you up out of it. God is simply removing the last little bit of impurity so that you may experience it in its fullness, for His glory!

This also includes former endeavors that went sour. As an example, I used to make a lot of money in business, but circumstances happened to cause me to lose my businesses. Of course, that is how I wound up in ministry, so IAM sure that God orchestrated it! Anyway, the Lord has been encouraging me to pick up that mantle again, the mantle of business, but this time to allow Him to operate it, using His ideas and His processes. His ideas are different than mine were. He has been showing me some things, building upon what I have already been doing for Him. The Master builder is at it again!

Just like for me, he has plans to bless you and prosper you (Jer. 29:11)! He is working in your life to bring you to that place of overflowing fruitfulness. Allow Him work in your life and remove the last little bit of dross. It will be well worth the effort!

CHAPTER THREE

God Is Building, Fashioning and Molding

Several times recently I have had the name "Coniah" resonate in my spirit. This morning I asked the Lord to tell me what He wanted to say.

I knew already that Coniah was a shortened version of the name Jehoichin, son of Jehoikim, one of the kings in the old testament. I also knew the prophet Jeremiah was tied in somehow too, but that is really all I knew. Mostly I remembered the Bible TV show version of the king Jehoichin whose sons were murdered in front of him and his eyes gouged out by Nebuchadnezzar the Babylonian king. Actually, I thought of king Coniah in a pretty negative light.

So, as I studied the name "Coniah" this morning, I was really surprised that the very first thing I saw was **"Yah is creating"**!

It was then I heard God say, **"I am building, fashioning and molding!"**

God is the master builder. He is creating right now, creating something new, creating something good out of the bad, creating the new wine for the new wineskins (Mk. 2:22). We all know it, we all feel it. We are yet to know what "it" looks like! But we know it's coming, and quickly. It's very exciting to know that Yah is creating!

He is building on an existing foundation.

Here's even more good news – God always builds on an existing foundation! If your foundation is solid, He can build on it. "[12] But if anyone builds on the foundation with gold, silver, precious stones, wood, hay, straw, [13] each one's work will be clearly shown [for what it is]; for the day [of judgment] will disclose it, because it is to be revealed with fire, and the fire will test the quality *and* character *and* worth of each person's work. [14] If any person's work which he has built [on this foundation, that is, any outcome of his effort] remains [and survives this test], he will receive a reward (1Cor. 3:12-14 Amp.)."

God has already checked your foundation in the last season. You may not even have realized it, but it has been weighed and measured, tested, poked, prodded, bent, stretched and pulled! You may even feel like the "crash-test dummy"! He did all of this because He needed you to know what your foundation was made of. You needed to go through the "day of judgement" (tests) because you needed *and still need* to know "what you're made of" – that you are, in fact, THE RIGHT STUFF! Now, just trust and believe that God is going to build on what He has already started!

He is ready to build on what He has already established in your life! Now you will receive more Gold (Revelation), more Silver (Wisdom), and more Precious Stones - Spiritual Gifts, Treasures, Anointing, Inheritances and all the things that are of God! All the good stuff is coming! Believe it!

God also said He is FASHIONING.

Although the word "fashioning" is similar to "molding", it has a subtle difference. True, it means to give a particular shape or form to something, or to make something. But it also means to accommodate, adjust and adapt to fit! In other words, it means to "tweak" or fine-tune.

If your foundation is just slightly out of whack, out of alignment, out of kilter – God will be FASHIONING it. He will be adjusting and adapting your situation to make sure that your foundation is ready to build upon this year. It's just a minor tweak, a slight change in your attitude or the words that are coming out of your mouth. Maybe it's a minor paradigm shift or changing a mindset. Whatever it is, He will surely be fashioning your foundation in this season. He will have His completed temple, and He is ready to build (1Cor. 3:16)! Trust Him, rest in Him, relax in His faithful arms and be ready for a quick work!

He is also MOLDING!

However, the Lord said He is BUILDING, FASHIONING and MOLDING. That means that if your existing foundation isn't strong enough, the correct size, shape or height right now for Him to build upon, He will MOLD it into what it needs to be. To mold means that He will work it into the required shape or form so that He can continue building! Molds usually require a rigid or solid structure into which the material to be shaped must be placed. So, if you are not quite ready for God to build on your existing foundation, He is already working on the mold into which to place you! You may already be in it, since this is such a time of acceleration.

He will finish building what He has begun! He counted the cost before He started, and then He paid it! I guarantee He will finish the good work that He has begun in you! (Lk. 14:28, Phil. 1:6) Trust Him to do it now!

Welcome to the New Thing in the New Year! What you have counted as treasure in seasons past is what He will make more of available to you, and continue to pour out and lavish on you this year. Well done, thou good and faithful servant!

CHAPTER FOUR

Marching Through The Door To More. Get In Order According To Matthew 12:34! Go Supernatural.

A month or so ago I had a vision during Praise and Worship of THOR in a business suit marching through a door way. The name "Thor" literally means *THUNDER*! As I was witnessing this, I distinctly heard the Lord say, "Marching through the door to More!" I knew that He intended it for this upcoming season.

Now is the month for MORE – more of everything! He even gave me some keys to open the Door to More out of the book of Matthew, specifically Matthew 12:34 – where everything is in order!

However, the Lord started off in Matthew 17:24. In this passage of scripture, Peter ran into a situation where he needed some money. As soon as he got home (to Jesus), here is how the Bible says the conversation went:

"Jesus spoke to him about it FIRST, saying, "WHAT DO YOU THINK, Simon (emphasis mine)?"

What is interesting is that Jesus called Peter SIMON. Just the chapter before, in Matthew 16:18 Jesus had renamed him Peter (*petros,* which means "a piece of rock; a stone; a single stone; movable, insecure, shifting, or rolling).

I don't think Jesus changed His mind. There is a reason that He called him by the name Simon. The name Simon has a root of "hearing", or "one who has heard" and "one who hears". Jesus was fond of saying, "*Let him who has ears to hear…*" (Rev. 2:7). I believe Jesus was saying to him, "Listen up! You have heard the truth!" or "Pay attention! Hear Me now!" I believe Jesus is still saying it to us today!

The scripture reads that **Jesus SPOKE FIRST** about the situation. The blood spoke first, and it is still speaking today (Heb. 12:24)! Before any bill shows up in your mailbox, before any sudden sickness happens, **before *any situation in your life presents itself to you,*** God is ALWAYS there first! It is worth saying again! Before ANYTHING HAPPENS IN YOUR LIFE, HE IS THERE FIRST! He is the Alpha and the Omega (Rev. 1:8)! He knows the end from the beginning (Is. 46:10)!

Remember during the feeding of the five-thousand, "*Jesus looked up then, and seeing that a vast multitude was coming toward Him, He said to Philip, Where are we to buy bread, so that all these people may eat? But He said this to prove (test) him, **for He well knew what He was about to do*** (John 6:5-6 AMPC)."

Here is KEY #1: Jesus asked Simon (Peter) what he THOUGHT -- reminding him by the usage of his very name Simon, a name which means that he has already heard the answer -- because as a man thinketh in his heart (Prov. 23:7) out of the fullness of his heart he will speak (Matt. 12:34). What's in your heart? Because that is what is going to come out of your mouth!

Peter was given the opportunity at that first crucial, critical instant, before he opened his mouth to talk about it - to either go

NATURAL or **SUPERNATURAL** with what came out of his mouth next!

I believe today that God is giving us the exact same opportunity! God is saying to all of us Simons, first of all, "YOU HAVE HEARD THE TRUTH! REMEMBER WHAT I HAVE SAID!" and next, "What do you THINK ABOUT it (your current predicament)? What is going to come out of your heart – and your MOUTH?"

"For out of the fullness (the overflow, the superabundance) of the heart the mouth speaks (Matt 12:34 AMPC)."

When we are faced with IMPOSSIBLE circumstances that are beyond our control – sudden huge bills, car wrecks, emergency room visits, family relationships that explode, chronic sickness and disease -- do you automatically go **NATURAL**, and *think*, "How in the WORLD am I going to take care of (fill in the blank)?" I caution you to be very careful about what comes out of your mouth next!

Key #2: GO SUPERNATURAL! Remember Matthew 12:34 (1, 2, 3, 4)! Get in order and let God take care of it! Because if it's impossible, you can't do it anyway! IMMEDIATELY GIVE GOD GLORY and thank Him for taking care of the issue! Because YOU are not going to! Not in THIS world, anyway.

Further, Jesus asked Peter, "*Do **earthly rulers** collect duties **or tribute** from **their own sons** or from 'others not of their own family*' (Matt. 17:25 AMPC, emphasis mine)?" The Aramaic translation of this phrase means, "strangers". **<u>Strangers</u>**? YES! We are not just STRANGERS, we are ALIENS!

"Beloved, I implore you as aliens and strangers and exiles [in this world] to abstain from the sensual urges (the evil desires, the passions of the flesh, your lower nature) that wage war against the soul. (1 Peter 2:11)"

Now, don't miss this! That is why the rulers, the powers and principalities of this WORLD (Eph. 6:12) want us to pay them tribute -- because we are in it, but not of it (John 17:16)! We are NOT OF THEIR FAMILY! We do not have their DNA! We have the DNA of our heavenly Father! They are trying to get us to **pay them tribute by opening our mouths**, giving them credit as well as the ability to take away our future! Your future is valuable to the Kingdom and they are out to steal it! Your words are extremely POWERFUL! They are the building blocks of creation! Do not use them to pay tribute (duties, taxes) and give credit to the enemy!

Key #3: Next, Jesus, having the voice of many waters (EX. 43:2) says several things simultaneously as He declares to Simon (Peter), "**THEN THE SONS ARE EXEMPT** (Matt. 17:26)". We are **aliens**, but we are also sons! This is where my vision of Thor in a business suit comes in. We are Sons of Thunder (Mark 3:17) busy about the Father's business, marching through the door into the MORE of God's heavenly realms of power! He is teaching us and showing us how! He is getting us into order – MARCHING ORDER -- 1, 2, 3, 4!

We are EXEMPT! Jesus said so! We don't have to pay! Listen, **Jesus has already paid the price IN FULL!** He has already paid the tribute! He has paid the duties and the taxes, the price for us to be free! Don't pay any more! Do not use your words to pay tribute to the enemy any longer! March through the door to MORE! Get in order according to Matthew 12:34 (1, 2, 3, 4)!

Here is the take-away for Marching through the Door to More – speak life. Remember Matthew 12:34 - Get into order and Do NOT open your mouth unless you have something life-filled and positive to say, full of the Glory of God! DO NOT UTTER ANOTHER NEGATIVE WORD!

Remember the widow woman whose child had died, the Shunnamite woman who sought out Elisha immediately upon the child's demise. She left to find Elisha (to seek God), saying NOTHING about the child's 'natural' death, even to her husband.

SHE WENT SUPERNATURAL! Her responses to Elisha's questions through Gehazi were all the same -- "All is Well!"

"Run at once to meet her and say to her, 'Is all well with you? Is all well with your husband? Is all well with the child?'" And she answered, "All is well. (2 Kings 4:26)"

Even though her child was dead at home in his bed in the natural, her powerful, life-filled words were enough to invoke a response from "The Man of God", for God to move on her behalf and resurrect him from the dead! She did NOT give the enemy credit for killing her boy. She didn't speak a single negative word!

Our God is the same yesterday, today and forever! He moved on the Shunnamite woman's behalf, and He will move on yours! He will send help, He will fill up your jars of oil and He will resurrect your loved ones from death and Hades back into life! He has the Keys, and He has given them to YOU – your WORDS!

Remember, ALL IS WELL. You have a God who loves you and wants to bless you and keep you. He is the maker of heaven and earth! He can do anything and He wants to do it for you! He has given you the POWER of your words! Use the POWER of your words to speak life into your situations and circumstances, decree breakthrough in the face of natural disaster, and you will see the manifestation of Marching through the door to More!

God Speaks

CHAPTER FIVE

I Heard A Voice Say: "Follow Me!"

A Vision of the King

During praise and worship at church recently, God kept telling me to "sit down." I heard Him say it several times, so realizing that it was Him saying it and not my tired body, I did. When I finally did I had an encounter – an amazing vision of the Lord Jesus.

I saw the face of God. His eyes were sunken deep in His face, penetrating and staring straight at me. His eyes looked like lion's eyes. Then in the vision, His face turned into the face of a lion.

Next I saw a dark tunnel and I was standing over it, looking down and into it. In the vision I remember thinking it looked like a scene from "Future World", the scene where the young man went down into the tunnel on the riverboat at the amusement park. It was very dark. There were dim lights on either side of this tunnel, much like the "tunnel of love". I stood over it, staring into this deep, dark tunnel.

Suddenly I saw a raging fire, bright orange and red with a platform ablaze behind the outline of a guitar player. I could only make out the silhouette of him playing with the fire raging brightly behind him. Just then, Jesus emerged from the flames. He was dressed all in white, wearing His King's crown. He walked straight toward me out of the flames, striding in slow motion, staring right at me. His eyes penetrated my heart and pierced my soul.

He continued to walk past me, and as He did I saw His face close-up. It was the face of a young man. He appeared to be just a young kid, maybe in His 20s. He had dirty smudges on His face in places and His crown was tilted forward onto His forehead, almost covering one eye, as if He had been in a fight.

As He stared at me, never taking His eyes from mine, His attire became that of a modern army combat soldier. His crown had changed into a green army helmet, still slanted on His forehead, and His face still had those same dirty smudges on it. His eyes never left mine until He was completely past me. I even saw His green backpack as He strode by in slow motion.

Once He had passed me, I could see Him from behind and He was now dressed in full Kingly armor. I could see His shoulders and the back of His helmet – He was wrapped in metal. He stood more than a head taller than the crowd behind Him. As He continued His trek, I could see the back of His King's armor.

It was then that I heard a voice say, "FOLLOW ME!"

That shocked me, and in the vision I jumped, startled. There was a crowd following behind Him, a huge throng, from the oldest saints to the youngest – the oldest in the Lord from thousands of years ago to the present of those who had recently passed. The oldest saints were in a sort of a haze, a fog or a cloud, and I couldn't really make them out in their robes. The youngest of those behind Him were sharp and clear, and I could see their blue jeans and their sandals.

I fell into line behind Him, and I heard the words, "Rank and File." The thought went through my head in the vision, "Fall into place," then "Fall into rank." At that point in the vision I said to myself, "FOLLOW ME!"

God responded, "Someone IS following you! Somebody will ALWAYS FOLLOW YOU, no matter what you are teaching. What are you discipling them into?"

He is right, of course. Anybody who is feeding the sheep has followers. The question is, what are we discipling our "followers" into? We need to feed them the truth, the Word and nothing more.

Our King Fights For Us and Into Battle!

God loves "THREES". He loves the number THREE: Father, Son, Holy Spirit; Jesus rose on the third day; and past, present, future. He showed me three different images of Himself in this vision. In the first one at the beginning of the vision I believe the Lord was showing Himself as He is when we are first saved; the King that rescues us from the flames of Hell.

A closer look into the Kingdom, however, will show that our King fights for us, as shown by His off-kilter crown and the dirty smudges on His face. He also showed Himself as the One that still fights for us today, the army troop, He's our soldier. Finally, He is our soon-coming King...He is our Captain of the guard, our leader into the end-times war, with the battle cry, "FOLLOW ME!"

The term "rank and file" relates to the rows and columns of individual foot-soldiers, the troops that follow the leader into battle. I believe the Lord is calling us to get into rank and file – get into proper position in the army of the Lord, into our proper RANK and CALLING. Not until we do this can we answer His battle cry and follow Him into battle! If we are out of position, we are ill-equipped to do what needs to be done on the battlefield.

In some situations, there are people who are blocking others, failing to yield the "right of way". They are hogging the podium or may be controlling individuals who are afraid of competition. They may be afraid of losing money in the offering tray. They won't let the sheep go out and minister, in essence, refusing to allow others to mature in the Lord. They need to get out of the way! Jesus said about the Pharisees in Matthew 23:13, "You won't go in yourselves, and you don't let others enter either!"

Those that have failed to step up into position need to do so! Both of these circumstances are slowing everybody else down! We ALL need to be prepared and in our proper positions, trained up and filled up, ready to do battle and wage war for the Kingdom of God. If we are out of position, what are we teaching those who are following us?

Be in Proper Position

I was impressed by the raging inferno and the guitar player on the platform at the beginning of the vision. I believe the Lord was saying that it is our WORSHIP – our PRAISE – that brings us into the proper position. It is our praise that correctly positions us to be with Him. I believe that when we are "on fire" for Him, when we burn for Him, when we worship Him, He longs to be with us as well.

He speaks to us during worship. We learn about Him and ourselves in relation to Him and others during worship! It is our praise that calls to Him. His own Word says, "Call to Me and I will answer you (Jer. 33:3)." He also says, "Draw near to Me, and I will draw near to you" (James 4:8). He answers praise. In fact, He INHABITS it (Ps. 22:3)! He gives us visions during worship – like this one! He gives prophetic words during worship – like this one! He speaks to His people during Worship – just like this!

If you are lacking anything in any way and desire it of the Lord, WORSHIP Him. Spend time every single day in submissive worship to our God and our King. It is the ONLY WAY to get into the proper position, ready to FOLLOW HIM.

CHAPTER SIX

God is Moving Us to a New Place

He Has Moved You to a New Place!

Have you ever moved to a new place, a new house, or a new apartment? In the new place, the rooms may not be in the same spots. If you head to the bathroom in the middle of the night and walk the way you have always gone in the past, you may end up running into a wall! Have you ever done that? Or stubbed your toe because something was in a different place, because you didn't "expect" it to be there...you expected something else instead?

When you move to a new place, whether it's a new city, a new state, or even just a new house, you must re-learn how to get around. You will take different roads to get to it. You may take different highways, different paths, and you will definitely be parking in a different place! You will be resting in a different place; you will be walking in new pathways.

The same is true in the spiritual realm! Once God moves you to a new place, the old paths and ways simply don't work anymore! If you continue to try to go the same way as you always have, you will stub your toe! You will run into walls and possibly even dead ends.

God is saying today that He has moved you to a new place! You no longer reside where you used to in the spirit realm. You *must* seek Him for new ways to do things and new pathways to get to where He wants you to go. The old way, the old paths you used to trod – the *comfortable* ways, the ones you are used to – simply will not produce the results that are desired by the Great I AM in this next season.

You Need New "Expectors"!

God is also saying you need new "expectors"! Recently I went to pay an honorarium to a speaker from one of my conferences. The speaker thanked me, but said, "I didn't expect anything." I said, "Well, you need some new expectors!"

See, you must expect good things – GOD things – in this new season. God is out to bless you! Disregard the doom and gloom message that is being belched out everywhere you go. God has measured you, and weighed you, and you have *not* been found wanting (see Daniel 5:27)!

YES! He is sifting everything, and it's going to shake, rattle, and roll! *Yes!* We are accelerating quickly toward the end, and judgment is coming on the world, however, please don't forget...**God is on your side** (see Romans 8:31)! In talking about the Holy Spirit, Jesus said, "...about judgment [the certainty of it], because the ruler of this world (satan) has been judged and condemned" (John 16:11 AMP).

You have not been judged! Satan has! And he's the "World's Biggest Loser!" You were already found righteous by the Righteous Judge (see Psalm 7:11) when you said "Yes!" to Jesus! You win!

So, listen! We must be smarter in this season than we have ever been. **Ask God!**

We must be more discerning than we have ever been. **Ask God!**

We must be more watchful and on guard, because we are at a new level spiritually – higher than we have ever been before! **Trust Holy Spirit!**

We are at a new place! We cannot continue to do things as they were done in seasons past, because they don't work anymore. We must rely on the Spirit of God in us! Listen to Him and trust Him, our witness.

And **expect good things!** Because they are coming!

John 16:13 (AMPC) But when He, the Spirit of Truth (the Truth-giving Spirit) comes, He will guide you into all the Truth (the whole, full Truth). For He will not speak His own message [on His own authority]; but He will tell whatever He hears [from the Father; He will give the message that has been given to Him], and He will announce and declare to you the things that are to come [that will happen in the future].

CHAPTER SEVEN

STAGES

I have felt really separated recently – cut off actually. It is as if God is pruning people out of my life and it hurts! These are my friends, family and ministry associates that I have "grown up" with, people that I LOVE! In addition I have been experiencing issues recently with hurting people unintentionally, offending people unintentionally, and misunderstandings. Discussing these things with my husband yesterday as we went for a walk, I cried out to the Lord, asking Him, "WHY am I struggling with this at this stage in my ministry?" I didn't realize it then, but my question was also my answer!

See, since yesterday morning I have been hearing "STAGES....STAGES" in my spirit. First, I overheard my musician husband yesterday speak to another musician on the phone about stages, and it has been rolling around in me since then. This morning I was in the word, working on messages for my upcoming conferences. Again I heard, "Stages…Stages" in my spirit. My messages need to be about supernatural keys to unlock supernatural doors, so I discounted what I was hearing. But it still wouldn't go away!

So, thinking there was some kind of correlation between KEYS and STAGES I started researching the Hebrew language, as it is a code-cracker for all things Biblical. I researched stages online in Hebrew, then stages of the Hebrew language leading to stages of the Jewish life cycle, but nothing resonated. The whole time on the back of my mind was 'rocket', and something I remembered about the boosters that drop off. Suddenly, I heard "STAGES" loudly in my spirit, and realized that STAGES are part of the rocket deployment process!

Researching that, I found there are typically four stages from rocket ship deployment to actual accomplishment of its goal. This is where I realized that my question was actually my answer – and for some that are reading this it is yours, too!

STAGE ONE: Lift-off – Launching your career or your ministry. In preparing for Lift-off you had to get to the launching site. The launching site is the place where you continuously met with the Lord. This is why you have heard God request that you meet Him in a "certain place"… just like Abraham did in Gen. 19:27, Jacob did in Gen. 28:16 ("…surely the Lord is in this place…"), Moses did with the 'tent of meeting' in Ex.33:7, and Jesus did by going to solitary places in Mark 1:35. You studied to show yourself approved. You yielded to God. You met with God on His terms so He could craft you into a vessel -- the ROCKET -- that He could use to deliver a specific payload. He maneuvered you into position, fully yielded to Him and ready to launch. The FIRES burned, excitement reigned and then it was, "HOUSTON…We have Lift-off!!" Woohoo!

Then came the **FIRST STAGE SEPARATION** -- You set out on your own, officially launched, whether in business or ministry. Your mentor or other encouragers and early supporters in your endeavors were separated from you. You may have had a select few accompany you. After all, not everyone can go to the top of the mountain, right? Some have to stay at the base camp. These that were left served a holy purpose, and hopefully they are mature enough to know that they were used of the Lord and they don't feel used by you!

In my research I found this definition (credit www.fas.org) for "LAUNCH VEHICLES":

"Most current launch vehicles consist of two or more rockets or stages that are stacked on top of each other. The second stage (YOU) is on top of the first (YOUR MENTOR, PASTOR, TEACHER, etc.), and so on. The first stage is the one that lifts the rocket off the launch pad and is sometimes known also as a "booster" or "main stage". When the first stage runs out of propellant <u>or has reached the desired altitude and velocity, its rocket engine is turned off and it is separated</u> so that the subsequent stages do not have to propel unnecessary mass. Dropping away the useless weight of stages whose propellant has been expended means less powerful engines can be used to continue the acceleration, which means less propellant has to be carried, which in turn means **more payload can be placed into orbit** (emphasis mine)."

Did you catch that? MORE PAYLOAD CAN BE PUT INTO ORBIT! Listen! Human beings didn't come up with this stuff! God did! Come on, Main Stages, Thruster Rockets, Boosters! You are LAUNCHING GOD'S ROCKETS! It's about the Payload!

SECOND STAGE SEPARATION - Fairing Separation – A fairing is used to protect a satellite or other payload (YOU, YOUR MINISTRY and/or CAREER) during launch. These "FAIRINGS" are the people that you took WITH YOU up the mountain! These are those that God sent with you to protect you, exhort you, support you and help you. However, there is no longer any need for these FAIRINGS. He is your protection (Ps. 59:9), your vindicator (Job 19:25), your justifier (Rom. 3:26 NKJV) and your shield (Ps. 5:12).

According to my research this morning, this second stage separation occurs while the rocket is traveling at a pace literally faster than a speeding bullet! This means that while you are ministering -- during your ACCELERATION – you may be getting ready to be separated again! Can somebody say PRUNING?

That is why it hurts so much, because it's pruning! God is cutting away the GOOD to make room for the BEST. He requires the very best, strongest and fastest rockets to deliver His Godly payloads! As a prophet, I know that if I am experiencing it, others are or will be as well. There is nothing uncommon to the body. This means I know for certain that there are times in your life and in your ministry that God will set you into position and launch you seemingly just to separate you -- repeatedly -- over and over, until you deliver His payload that you are carrying!

I have to realize that at certain times I am the main stage and not **ON** the main stage! Sometimes I am the "booster rocket", and sometimes I am the "fairing". I am NOT always the satellite! And neither are you! You are used of the Lord to perform His good pleasure!

"...for it is God who is at work in you, both to will and to work for His good pleasure." Phil. 2:13 NASB

Sometimes you are delivering the payload, and other times you will be helping others to deliver theirs! Either way, it's God's will, and you are smack-dab in the middle of it.

LAST STAGE SEPARATION: Payload Separation – When you deliver the goods, or accomplish whatever it is that God has instructed you to do, for His glory. This would be whatever God created you to be and to do – Evangelist, Teacher, Mother, Prophet, Administrator, Waiter, Real Estate Investor...

This is where you deliver the gift of eternal Life, teach about Him, love with His love, prophesy about Him, administrate His works, serve them up, invest in His Kingdom or whatever God has called you to deliver on His behalf...Kingdom Payload in the Name of Jesus.

It may hurt for a short time to be pruned. However, God knows exactly what you need to become the very best rocket you can possibly be. He also knows who else needs you to become the very best so that they can become the very best that they can be, too! He will align you and re-align you until your payload and theirs is delivered. So, THRUST!

CHAPTER EIGHT
The Action Center And A Pattern For Revival

I should know by now that when something happens over and over to me that God is speaking. As usual, Jehovah-Sneaky took me by surprise. No one can tell me He doesn't have a supernatural sense of humor!

Over the last couple of months, I have had more computer issues than ever before in my lifetime. It has been a major battle just to keep a computer running as laptop after laptop has crashed, gotten viruses or just flat out died. In fact, the one I was using for this message has an issue with heat – it runs at such a high temperature that the bottom of it burns the skin and is too hot to touch. Needless to say, it's impossible to use the way it was designed – on top of a lap!

Getting creative, I propped it up on stacks of coasters on the kitchen table to let some of the heat escape and turned it on. What happened next really surprised me! A screen popped up that I have never seen before: **The Action Center**. This stunned me because I didn't ask for any help troubleshooting this problem. However, I laughed as I read the "HELP" options on this computer screen. Once again I realized that God has an incredible sense of humor and will use whatever He deems necessary to make His point. *(Photo via Pixabay)*

Seeking a Pattern for Revival

You see, I have been studying Revival. Not just studying it for information, but earnestly looking for a template and seeking a pattern to follow. We all know that God is a 'pattern God', right?

As an example, He gave us the BIBLE to follow – our owner's manual. He gave us Jesus as our mentor and our example to follow here in the earth realm and beyond. He gave us the template of prayer in Matthew 6:9-13, the Lord's Prayer. There are other patterns also, including Solomon's temple and Noah's Ark.

I understand that He does not need to do anything the same way twice, but sometimes He does anyway! Knowing this, I was looking for a pattern, an example to follow so I could encourage others to do the same. In particular I have been studying the Azusa Street Revival. I am concurrently reading a Frank Bartleman book of the account, William J. Seymour's sermons and the 1906-1908 newsletters that were sent out by the Azusa ministry that set the world ablaze.

I was looking for a PATTERN, and I found one!

In researching all of these different sources, I learned that during revival people were saved, sanctified, filled with the Holy Spirit and received their tongues; they were fed, healed and set free from all different types of bondages, in particular religious spirits. They were released from their fleshly carnality and their pride melted away as they fell prostrate on the floor in the presence of God, sometimes for hours. Spirits fled as people were delivered of demons and all came to know the God of Heaven in unity with love, mercy and compassion for each other and all of mankind. **What I saw over and over again was that heart issues were resolved in Revival!**

Recently I was in Mark reading about Jesus feeding the four-thousand with seven loaves of bread and some fish (Mark

8:1-10). While reading this tribute to Jesus' compassion the Lord gave me a sudden epiphany about Revival: It is Jesus! He flashed a vision in front of me of Jesus walking the streets, preaching the Kingdom and healing all who followed Him. **I suddenly realized that JESUS is REVIVAL!**

Revival Requires Ridding the Flesh

Of course, I soon realized the key to becoming more like Jesus is to be less like...well, less like ME. Although God loves me He has pruned me down to a twig at times to get rid of heart issues – my flesh. As I recounted this observation to my husband, I realized what we need for Revival is a "flesh castration". Our flesh needs to become of no account – not able to reproduce, have no seed and therefore no fruit!

This is where the Action Center on my computer screen comes in! I have been asking God to open my eyes and ears to what He wants to reveal to me, both in His Word and in this earthly realm. It has been my sincere desire to go deeper with Him as He leads us all into Revival. So, when I started looking at the different options that my ailing computer offered me for fixing it, from the spiritual viewpoint of leading our hearts to revival, I just had to laugh with God. All the gold is His, all the silver is His, and every computer screen on earth is His. He used mine for His Glory today on the ACTION CENTER screen!

Action Center Screen

The Action Center screen listed multiple items that needed my attention. They are listed below as God showed them to me.

• **Review recent messages and resolve problems.** Have you been hearing from God? Have you heard any messages recently that really "hit home"? These messages have been sent to you directly from Abba. He is pinging your heart to make you more sensitive to the Holy Spirit, so that He can come in and clean up some issues and take you into Revival.

• **Action Center has detected one or more issues for you to review.** The Holy Spirit is our ACTION CENTER! Our Heavenly Father is bringing those issues front and center because He wants to get the problems resolved. You are His child and He wants you in step with Him, in Revival with Him! He is weeding the gardens of our hearts to remove the issues that keep us separated from Him. He wants us closer!

1. Security – No problems with security. Our salvation is secure.

2. Maintenance – No maintenance issues, either. We read the Word. We go to church. We may even be the Pastor or the house Prophet. Regardless, for some of us, there may be an intimacy that is lacking that God wants restored. He is taking the first steps to bridge the gap. Better check #3: "unreported problems".

3. Check for Solutions to unreported problems. There are problems on your computer that have not been reported. Some of these problems might have solutions available.

This is where the work really begins! God wants NOTHING between us and Him, in fact, Revival demands it! This is where some of us may skin our knees falling to them!

Is there any unrepented sin? Any secret sins? Rebellion? Disobedience? Anger? Dissatisfaction? These are "unreported problems." Just because we haven't spoken about them or confessed them doesn't mean they don't exist and that our Father in Heaven doesn't know about them! These "unreported problems" are creating distance, blocking the blessings of God.

However, please bear in mind, we have a choice here. Below this statement is an *IGNORE THIS MESSAGE* link, a *VIEW PROBLEMS TO REPORT* link, as well as a *CHECK FOR*

SOLUTIONS button. I don't think any of these need spiritual interpretation. However, simply by virtue of the fact that there ARE options it can mean only one thing:

We have a choice and free will. We can continue to ignore the issues or we can take a look at them. The only one who knows how to SOLVE what we see there is God. He is willing! Are we ready to come closer and step into revival? Let's report those problems, repent and be forgiven!*(Photo via Pixabay)*

4. Troubleshoot a problem with your computer's hard disk. The OS (Operating System) was unable to open a file on your computer's hard disk 4-times...Go online for troubleshooting steps.

God has been sending us messages, over and over, about our "HARD DISK"...in other words, our hard heart. He wants us to talk with Him about it, to "come up here" (Rev. 4:1). *Go Online for Troubleshooting Steps!* However, because we have free will, once again we have options to either *ARCHIVE* this message or *View Message details*. We are again given the opportunity to IGNORE or TAKE ACTION. God prefers we act and "come up here"! After all, 1 John 4:4 says that you are of God and have overcome because He who lives in you is greater than him who is in the world!

5. Set up Backup – This is the easiest step of all! Let's ask the Holy Spirit to be our "Back Up", to do the things that Jesus proclaimed that He sent Him to do! He sent Him to be our Comforter – Counselor, Helper, Advocate, Intercessor, Strengthener, Standby (John 16:7 AMPC). Simply ask Holy Spirit to open the eyes and ears of our understanding (Eph. 1:18, Mt. 13:13) and to lead us and guide us into all Truth (John 16:13)!

<u>Jesus is Revival!</u>

This Truth is Jesus and JESUS IS REVIVAL! We want

Revival and God wants to give it to us!

He will be all of these things and more as we choose to turn to Jesus in Revival! We all should do a heart-check today to begin to rid ourselves of any residual pride and other sins that still reside in us. We want to walk into Revival, the sooner the better! Let's all work together in Unity toward that end.

CHAPTER NINE

God Is Giving Us Bundles Of Blessings!

A Vision of Balloons

Recently I saw balloons of blessings in the spirit! As I prayed, a hole opened over me in the ceiling, and there were balloons hanging all around it. I reached up into the air and started pulling the balloons down. I pulled the first one down, but amazingly it was still up there and also in my hand! I kept pulling the balloons down over and over, but it didn't diminish their number! The balloons of blessings were still there around this hole in the ceiling, no matter how many I pulled down.

I pulled down the balloons in front of me and somehow I saw balloons behind me too, so I grabbed them as well! As I did I was pulling these balloons INTO me. I had balloon ribbons wrapped all around my hands; so many of them I couldn't hold them all! Then God wrapped them all up like a big flower bouquet and handed them to me! The rope of balloon ribbons was so big – an incredibly huge, beautiful vine! In my hands I had balloons of so many colors; silver metallic ones that shone so brightly, white and gold ones, multi-colored ones – **an exquisite display of the blessings of God!**

Let it Go!

I was holding this vine of ribbon strings very tightly against my chest, holding onto these balloons of blessings, when the Lord reminded me that His blessings are given to us to give to others. He said, "Let it go!"

I did, and I felt such a glorious freedom! The weight was gone from my chest; the weight of trying to hang onto these blessings of God! **My heart exploded inside of me from the joy and passion of the love that was just given away! God used me to give away His blessings!**

In this season, He will use you too! I believe that God has been speaking to all of us recently about the changes that are coming, and they are GOOD changes! **He is giving us bundles of blessings to be set free and given away to others. Trying to keep them all is too much work when He has so many available. No matter how many you choose to pull down from the heavenlies, their number will never be diminished! Give as much as you can, and then go back for more!**

God will even bundle them all up and give them to you at once! Be looking for bundles of blessings to arrive all at one time! He is not just giving you blessings from the future. He is even giving you the ones that are BEHIND you – blessings that you have missed out on from the past! He knows where they are and wants to bless you with them. Trust Him to do it!

Reach up, grab your blessings in prayer and then turn them loose on the world around you. You will feel so amazingly and gloriously free! **In this season, God wants you to have all of the blessings that He intended, even some from the past that didn't materialize. His purpose is to bless you and those around you.**

You will be carrying someone else's blessing! Don't hang onto the blessings of God. Give them away, and you will receive more – much more – in return! He has an unending supply. Instead, seek Him, then simply reach up and grab some more!

CHAPTER TEN

Singularity – Three Headlights

A Sign: Single Head Lights

Driving home the other night, I got on the freeway and saw a single headlight coming up behind me. Initially I thought it was a motorcycle, but soon realized that it was a car with a missing headlight. It actually gave me a scare initially, because I wasn't expecting a car. I quickly shrugged it off because it's not that uncommon in a major city like Houston to see cars with missing parts, from front ends to bumpers, so a headlight wasn't that unusual.

However, when I got closer to my house, I saw two more cars with only one headlight, literally back-to-back. Now THAT was unusual! I saw THREE cars with just one headlight on my drive home. As I pondered this event, I realized that God was speaking to me!

I asked the Lord, "God, what are You trying to tell me?" I didn't get an immediate response, but the "three headlights" encounter simply wouldn't leave me. I have been meditating on this for days, feeling the weightiness of this prophetic sign, praying and waiting for clarification from the Lord.

During worship recently I was taken into an encounter. The Lord said, "Come up here." As I focused on the light I saw with my eyes closed, it got brighter and brighter, and I saw the headlight of a car – a single headlight that was round and bright. The funny thing is that the headlight of the car I saw turned into the moon as I focused on it.

Next, I saw Jesus' hands, and I realized He was holding the moon. I saw Jesus seated, sitting cross-legged on the ground with the moon in His two hands. His face was lit up by the reflection of it, and He was beautiful! It occurred to me that Israel's calendar is set to the moon, and the moon is in Jesus' hands!

Focused, Singular Vision

During worship I also heard the word, "SINGULARITY." I had no idea what it meant, but I figured it had to do with the single-headlights. I looked it up as soon as I could, and found this:

The term Singularity has many definitions. The everyday English definition of Singularity is a noun that designates the quality of being one of a kind, strange, unique, remarkable or unusual. For a more specific definition of Singularity we can search The Wiktionary where we get the following: the state of being singular, distinct, peculiar, uncommon or unusual.

We, the people of God, are SINGULARITY! We are a peculiar people (1 Peter 2:9)! We are foreigners (1 Peter 2:11), strangers in a strange land! In Exodus 2:22, Moses names his son Gershom, for he said, "I have been a stranger in a strange land."

I also heard "head-lights", like a bulb came on in my head, as two separate words. I hadn't thought of them in that manner before, just as car parts – headlights, not Head-Lights! God was speaking about lights in my head, i.e., "the light bulb coming on!" **What I really think is that He wants us to get it through our heads that He is the Light!**

I felt in my spirit that we should really focus on Jesus, that He is the singular purpose for which God created us! I also felt strongly in my spirit that the Lord was saying for us to really FOCUS on Him and on our purpose – to have laser-sharp, FOCUSED SINGULAR VISION – that we are created for something SPECIFIC, for a special, singular PURPOSE.

A lot of us have been running around with a "shot-gun mentality" – if we do enough stuff, we're bound to hit something! **I believe that God wants us to stop and focus on what He is saying, find our purpose, and seek it for all we are worth with everything we have!**

Three Combined into One - Singularity

It also came to me during the encounter that the number three is significant, as is the number one. One stands for God, and three is the Trinity, us conforming to the image of Christ. As I soaked in the Lord's presence, He began to show me that the number three and the number one all work together – Father, Son and Holy Spirit – all in one God! He went on to give me multiple examples – one sun, one moon, one earth, yet all three work in tandem. He mentioned there are many stars and many galaxies, but only one planet with life.

He explained that there is one King, one Queen (the Bride), and one Kingdom, yet they are inseparable. One body, one soul and one spirit comprise the whole man.

He also talked to me about the Tallit, as there was a man in front of me wearing a tallit; and as I watched him put it over his head for his prayer closet, I wished in my heart that I had one. Just as my head tilted forward to pray, I heard the Lord say, "You have one," as my hair fell around my face, forming my own personal tallit! The Word says that a woman's hair is her glory (1 Cor. 11:15)! I got the full revelation of that today – the light came on for me, giving me full clarity of this verse.

Lastly, speaking of His Light, His marvelous Light, I believe that

God is talking to us and saying He is our light! The Lord showed me the vision of Jesus' face reflecting the light of the moon, His prize Israel, shining brightly in His hands. I felt the Spirit say that just as the moon reflects the light of the sun, Jesus reflects the light of the Father, and we reflect the light of Jesus, as He holds us in His hands!

So the more unusual you are, the more peculiar you are, the more one of a kind, strange, unique, remarkable or unusual you are – the more you are His prize and the more you look like Him, reflecting His image!

Shine On!

ABOUT THE AUTHOR

Edie Bayer
Kingdom Promoters – Promoting the Kingdom of God
www.KingdomPromoters.org
www.EdieBayer.com
Edie@KingdomPromoters.org

Edie Bayer is an author, a speaker and travelling minister. Edie's primary call is to promote others that are ministering in the Kingdom of God, creating unity instead of a spirit of competition. Edie believes that we are to "complete and not compete"!

Edie can be found on TBN, and is a backup TV show host for two television programs on Destiny TV.

Edie is a frequent contributor to the Elijah List (www.ElijahList.com), Spirit Fuel (www.SpiritFuel.me), and Women of Impact Ministries (www.womenofimpactministries.com).

Edie believes that EVERYBODY has a book in them – and it's TIME to write it! Her most recent assignment from God is to help other Christian authors pen their novels and texts. She helps budding authors accomplish their goals with her workshop entitled, **"Write That Book! You Have a Book in You – Now Write It!"** Edie teaches this workshop by invitation around the country.

Edie is co-founder of Kingdom Promoters (www.KingdomPromoters.org) along with her husband Darryl Bayer. Kingdom Promoters is a 501(C)(3) Non-Profit Organization. Kingdom Promoters' mission statement is "To promote the Kingdom of God, and to promote the people who promote the Kingdom of God!" This ministry works to further God's Kingdom by acting as an incubator to assist fledgling ministries in their start-up stages and promote those who are promoting the kingdom of God. Kingdom Promoters also hosts itinerant speakers and travelling ministers.

Please visit www.KingdomPromoters.org for more information about Edie Bayer, books, CD's and DVD's, as well as how to bring Edie to your church, fellowship, retreat, ministry or group!

GOD SPEAKS

www.ingramcontent.com/pod-product-compliance
Lightning Source LLC
Chambersburg PA
CBHW072037060426
42449CB00010BA/2313